# A Note to Paren

DK READERS is a compelling program for beginning readers, designed in conjunction with leading literacy experts, including Dr. Linda Gambrell, Distinguished Professor of Education at Clemson University. Dr. Gambrell has served as President of the National Reading Conference, the College Reading Association, and the International Reading Association.

Beautiful illustrations and superb full-color photographs combine with engaging, easy-to-read stories to offer a fresh approach to each subject in the series. Each DK READERS is guaranteed to capture a child's interest while developing his or her reading skills, general knowledge, and love of reading.

The five levels of DK READERS are aimed at different reading abilities, enabling you to choose the books that are exactly right for your child:

**Pre-level 1:** Learning to read
**Level 1:** Beginning to read
**Level 2:** Beginning to read alone
**Level 3:** Reading alone
**Level 4:** Proficient readers

The "normal" age at which a child begins to read can be anywhere from three to eight years old. Adult participation through the lower levels is very helpful for providing encouragement, discussing storylines, and sounding out unfamiliar words.

No matter which level you select, you can be sure that you are helping your child learn to read, then read to learn!

Penguin Random House

**Created by Leapfrog Press Ltd.**
**For Dorling Kindersley**
**Senior Editor** Linda Esposito
**Managing Art Editor** Peter Bailey
**US Editor** Regina Kahney
**Production** Josie Alabaster
**Picture Researcher** Liz Moore
**Illustrator** Mario Capaldi

**Reading Consultant**
Linda B. Gambrell Ph.D.

First American Edition, 1999
This edition, 2012
Published in the United States by DK Publishing
345 Hudson Street, New York, New York 10014


18 10 9 8 7 6 5 4 3 2
010–184579–July/2012


Published in Great Britain by Dorling Kindersley Limited.

A catalog record for this book is available from the Library of Congress.
ISBN: 978-0-7566-9297-1 (pb)
ISBN: 978-0-7566-9296-4 (plc)



Printed and bound in China.

The publisher would like to thank the following for their kind permission to reproduce their photographs:
Key: t=top, a=above, b=below, l=left, r=right, c=center
**Ancient Art & Architecture:** 4tl, 4bl; **Bridgeman Art Library:** 10tl; **Camera Press Ltd:** 34tl, 34bl, 36-7b; **Bruce Coleman Limited:** 18bl; **Coloursport:** 42tl; **Corbis UK Ltd:** 19b, 29b; **Gerry Cranham:** 2, 40-1b, 41tr, 42b, 45tl, 45br; **Dorling Kindersley Picture Library:** 40tl;/**Lynton Gardiner:** 5bl; **Lynton Gardiner/American Museum of Natural History:** 9; **Christi Graham/Nick Nicholls/British Museum:** 5tr; **Bob Langrish:** 7tr, 13tr, 17tr, 17cl, 32bl, 46t, 47tr, cr, br; **Karl Shone:** 46bl; **Jerry Young:** 10bl, 36bl, 37tr, 46br, 46-7b, 47bl, 49br; **AJ Drucker**, London 1932, portrait of AF Tschiffely: 12tl; **Mary Evans Picture Library:** 8b; **Herbert Graf**, Wien: 24-5, 27br, 30tl, 30bl; **Ronald Grant Archive:** 20bl, 21br, 23br, 31; **Houghton's Horses:** 44b; **Hulton Getty:** 23t, 45tr; **Image Bank:** 20tl; **Kobal Collection:** 21tl; **Bob Langrish:** 17tr, 28tr, 35br; taken from "Red Rum" by Ivor Herbert, **William Luscombe Ltd:** 39br; **Moviestore Collection:** 22b; **Peter Newark's Western Americana:** 6bl, br, 7br, 8tl, 8cl; **Only Horses:** 37cr, 38bl; **Pitkin Pictorials/ Household Cavalry:** 36tl; **Popperfoto:** 43; **Ruth Rogers**, Eire: 39trb; **John Slater:** 39tra; **South American Pictures:** 14lb; **Telegraph Colour Library:** 14tl; **Tony Stone Images:** 18tl, 35tr; **Topham Picturepoint:** 22tl; **Trip/F Good:** 33tr; **"Tschiffely's Ride", William Heinemann Ltd/Random House:** 12tl, 19tr; **Elisabeth Weiland:** 26tl, 27tr, 28bl, 29tr.
**Jacket image:** *Front:* **Gettyimages:** AllsportUK



# Contents

DK READERS

PROFICIENT 4 READERS

# Horse Heroes
## True Stories of Amazing Horses

Written by Kate Petty

DK

# Horses in history

**Pegasus**
In Greek mythology, Pegasus was a beautiful winged horse who became a constellation of stars in the sky.

People and horses have always had a special relationship. Ever since horses were first tamed and ridden 6,000 years ago, they have been admired for their intelligence, strength, and speed.

In ancient Greece, a beautiful, well-trained horse was the ultimate status symbol of kings and generals. The conqueror Alexander the Great was so proud of his brave horse Bucephalus (Byoo-SEFF-uh-luss), that he named a city after him.

*Statue of Alexander the Great riding Bucephalus in battle.*

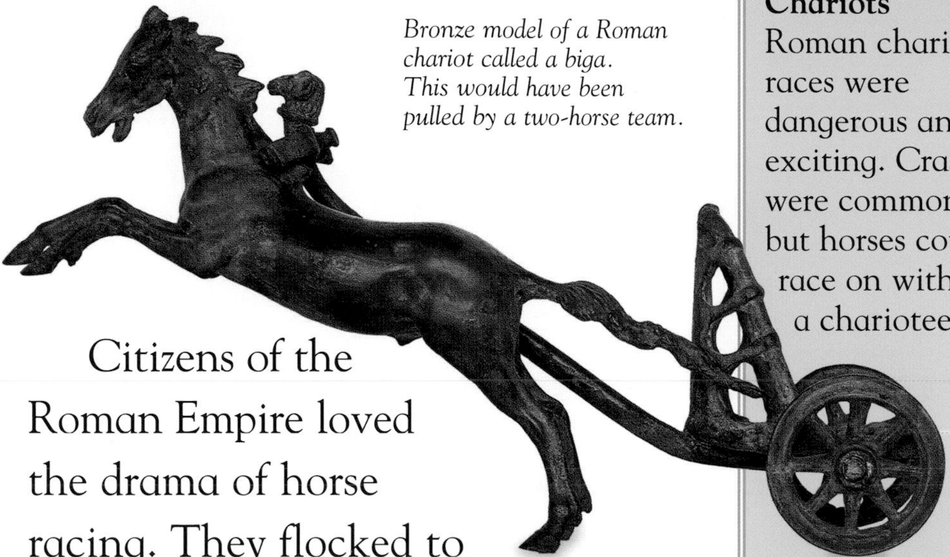

*Bronze model of a Roman chariot called a biga. This would have been pulled by a two-horse team.*

Citizens of the Roman Empire loved the drama of horse racing. They flocked to the arena to watch their favorite chariot teams thundering around the racetrack.

Horses were also important to Native Americans. The tribes of the Great Plains were expert horsemen and relied on horses for hunting buffalo and carrying warriors into battle.

Wherever people and horses have worked together, they have formed a loyal bond. This book tells the stories of some remarkable horses who have worked with their human partners to become heroes.

**Chariots**
Roman chariot races were dangerous and exciting. Crashes were common, but horses could race on without a charioteer.

**Racehorses**
Champion stallions were used for breeding during their racing years.

**Saddlebag**
Horses were very important to the Native American Dakota (Sioux) tribe. They were a favorite theme in Dakota art.

# Pony Express

When the little mustang came into view, the crowd began to clap and cheer.

Her rider, Johnny Fry, led her into the packed town square of St. Joseph, Missouri, that warm April evening in 1860. Johnny checked the mail pouch on the mustang's back for the last time as she snorted excitedly.

**Long journey** Pony Express riders took the mail 2,000 miles (3,200 kilometers) from Missouri to California.

*The cost of sending a letter on the Pony Express was worked out by weight. A letter cost $5 per ounce (28 grams).*

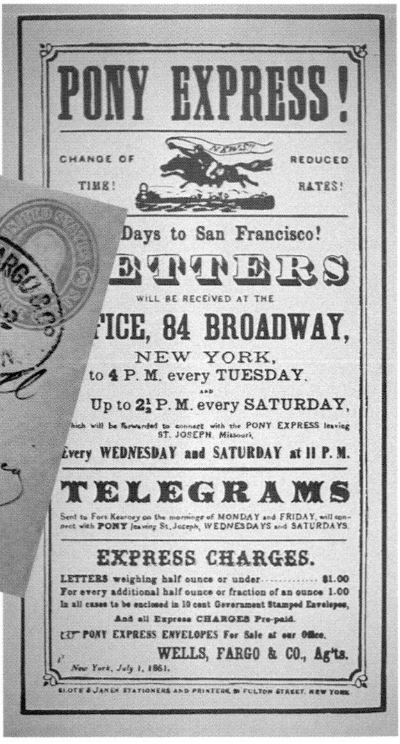


*This poster for the Pony Express service dates from 1861.*

**First delivery** Johnny Fry's mail sack held 49 letters and 3 newspapers.

A cannon boomed. They were away! The mustang raced off into the evening twilight, leaving the cheering crowds far behind.

Horse and rider had entered history as the first ever Pony Express team.

In 1860 there were no such things as telephones and fax machines. If you lived on the west coast of the United States, keeping up to date with the latest news on the east coast was almost impossible. It could take more than a month for mail to travel across the continent by wagon.

The Pony Express was a horse relay designed to keep the mail moving day and night. It cut down the time taken for mail to reach California to just eight days.

**Mustang**
This hardy breed is descended from the horses brought to America by Spanish explorers.

**Express riders**
Pony Express riders had to be under 18 years old and weigh less than 126 pounds (57 kilograms), so as not to slow down their horses.

Each horse and rider galloped at top speed to the next station. The rider leaped off the exhausted horse shouting "Pony rider coming!" The mail was transferred to a fresh horse and the rider galloped off again on his new mount.

There were 157 relay stations, and riders changed horses about six to eight times.

The teams risked death together on a daily basis.

**Transfer**
It took a rider two minutes to transfer between horses.

**Saddle up**
Mail pouches were sometimes sewn into the rider's saddle.

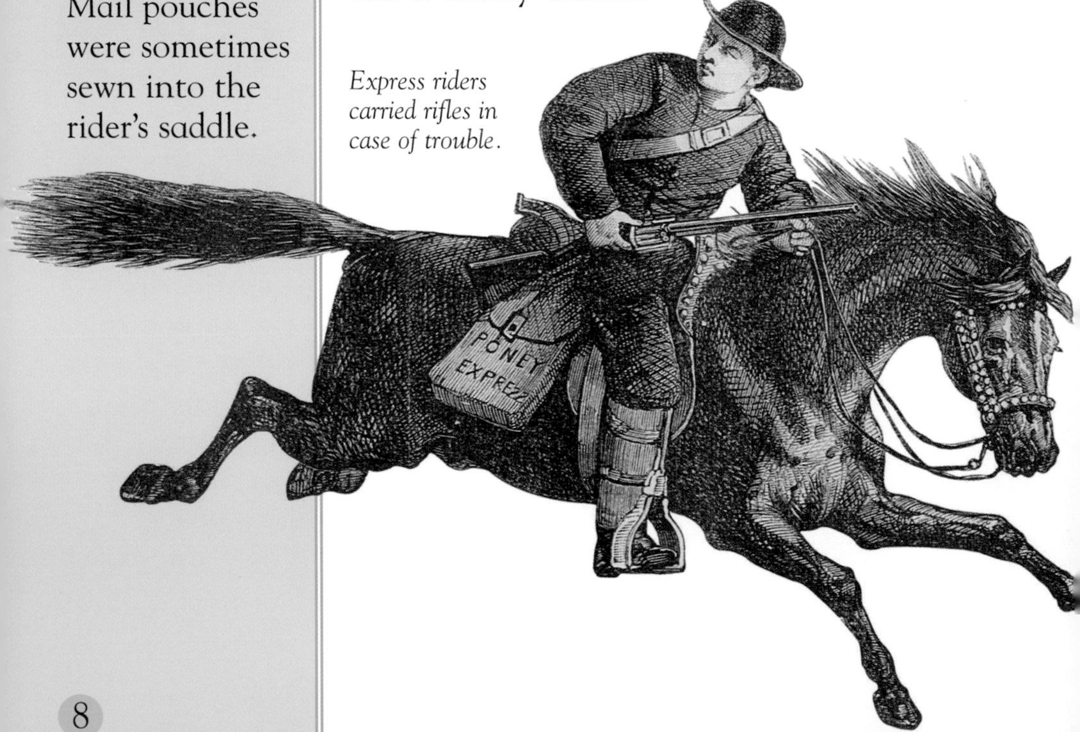


*Express riders carried rifles in case of trouble.*

Much of the route lay through the homelands of Native Americans, some of whom declared war on the white invaders of their territory.

One of the bravest riders was "Pony Bob" Haslam. In May 1860 he arrived at a station in Nevada to find the keeper dead and all the horses gone. He set out for the next station, which was 40 miles (64 kilometers) away.

"I knew I had to carry on. As I rode through the night, I kept watching my pony's ears. I knew he'd hear any Indian ambush before I did."

At the next station he persuaded the keeper to leave with them. Bob and his tireless horse saved the man's life—the next night, that station was attacked.

**Lethal weapon**
Several riders were wounded by Native American arrows but none were ever killed.

**Lincoln**
In 1860, Abraham Lincoln's first speech as U.S. President was carried by the Pony Express.

**Stagecoach**
The Pony Express closed down when the transcontinental telegraph system opened in 1861. Stagecoach operators Wells, Fargo & Company took over the route.

The Pony Express teams rode across rocky mountain passes and wide, empty plains in scorching sun, pouring rain, and freezing blizzards. If their rider fell off, some brave horses carried on alone to the next station.

The final stop was Sacramento, California. Crowds of eager people would gather to watch the arrival of the last rider on the route bringing them their mail and newspapers.

The success of the Pony Express teams proved that it was possible for the east and west coast to keep in touch. It was a milestone on the way to modern America. The horses and riders that ran the Pony Express were real pioneers.

The Pony Express is remembered today by horse lovers who ride the express's desert tracks for pleasure. Their journeys pay tribute to the riders of 1860, who insisted that "the mail must get through." ❖

WELCOME PONY EXPRESS
HOTEL

**Tschiffely**
Aimé Tschiffely (Ay-may Shiff-ell-ee) was a Swiss teacher living in Argentina.

**Americas**
Tschiffely wanted to ride from South to North America across the Panama Canal.

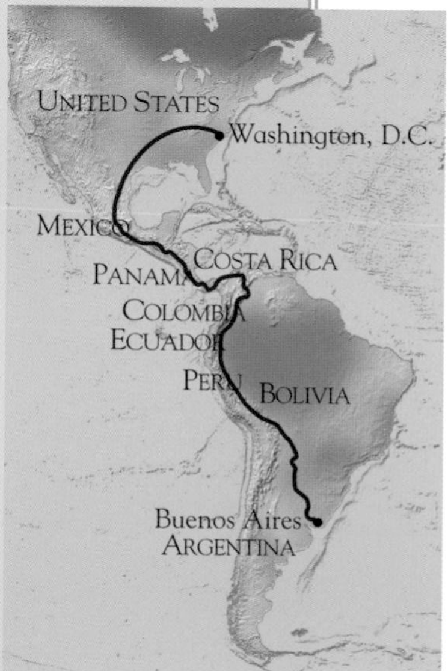


# Tale of two horses

When Tschiffely told people about his idea early in 1925, they thought he had gone mad.

"Impossible! It can't be done!"

Tschiffely wanted to be the first man ever to ride from Buenos Aires in Argentina all the way to Washington, D.C.

He realized that the 10,000-mile (16,000-kilometer) journey would be full of difficulties, but it had been his secret ambition for years.

Tschiffely knew that he needed two tough and resourceful horses if he was to succeed. He chose Gato and Mancha, Criollo horses aged 15 and 16. They had belonged to an Argentinian Indian chief and roamed free on the plains. They were not handsome and they were headstrong, but they knew how to survive in the wild.

Tschiffely and the horses set off in April 1925. After four months, the travelers crossed over into Bolivia.

In that time the trio had learned to trust each other and to work together as a team.

One day, as they rode along the shore of a lake in Peru they reached a shallow strip of water. Gato reared up and refused to go on.

An Indian rushed toward them, shouting that the water hid dangerous quicksand. He led them to a safe trail. Tschiffely was amazed. The horse had saved their lives!

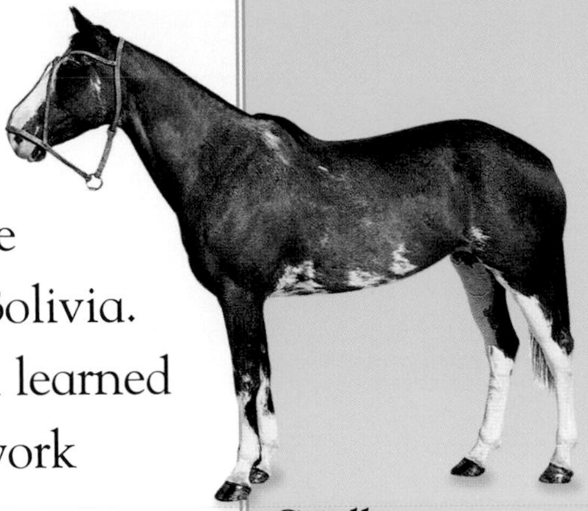

**Criollo**
These horses are very tough and can carry heavy weights over long distances.

**Horse sense**
People believe that horses have a sixth sense that warns them about danger.

**Andes**
The Andes stretch up to 20,000 feet (6,000 meters). They are pitted with sheer, rocky gorges.

**Rope bridge**
Andes natives have built thin rope bridges across gorges for centuries. Many people have to cross blindfolded because they are too scared to look down.

As they rode on through Peru, they began to climb the Andes—a huge range of snow-capped mountains.

One morning, they came across a sight that made Tschiffely's blood run cold. The way forward was along a rickety old rope bridge that stretched over a deep gorge. One slip would prove fatal.

Tschiffely and Mancha slowly began to cross. Tschiffely spoke to his horse in a quiet, calm voice, gently patting his haunches.

When they reached the middle, the bridge swayed violently. If Mancha panicked and turned back, they would both fall to their deaths. But Mancha waited calmly for the bridge to stop moving, then went on. When Gato saw his companions safe on the other side, he crossed the bridge as steadily as if he were walking on solid ground.

**Broken trail**
Constant rain in mountainous regions often causes muddy landslides.

From Peru, Tschiffely headed into Ecuador and followed a series of tracks through lush forests over high mountains and down into valleys.

At night, Tschiffely never tied up the horses. He knew they would not run. The three travelers were sharing a great adventure, each showing the others the way.

Zigzagging up a narrow trail one day, Tschiffely saw that the path ahead had been swept away by a landslide, leaving a sheer drop. There was no choice but to turn back and find another route. Tschiffely tightened Gato's packs to get ready for a long detour.

But Mancha had other ideas. Tschiffely saw with horror that Mancha was preparing to jump the gap. His heart rose in his mouth as Mancha sailed through the air and landed on the other side. The horse turned and neighed to his companions not to be afraid.

Tschiffely and Gato soon followed.

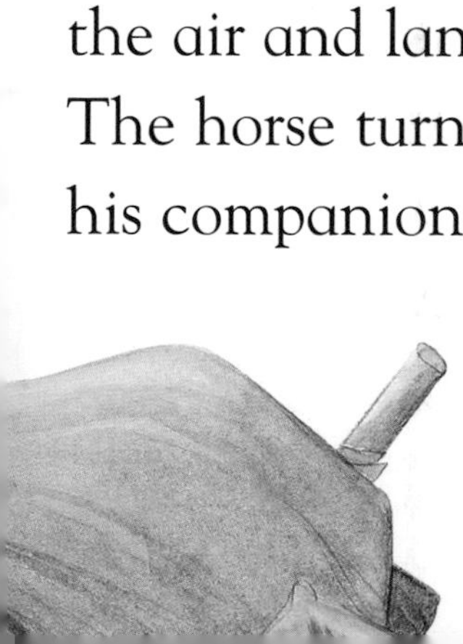

**Herd instincts**
Wild horses stay in groups, or herds. Mancha and Gato would instinctively follow each other, whatever the dangers.

**High jump**
Horses push off to jump from their back legs. Mancha was particularly brave, as the ground was very slippery.

**Dense jungle**
The jungles of Central and South America are home to some of the world's most dangerous snakes, such as the 30-foot (10-meter) anaconda.

**Crocodile**
Horses seem to remember that their ancestors were hunted by crocodiles, and know to be afraid of them.

As their adventure stretched on, the three travelers reached the Panama Canal and crossed into Costa Rica and then Mexico.

Moving through dense jungle, the trio had to cope with mosquito bites and attacks by vampire bats and poisonous snakes.

Once, Mancha slipped into a crocodile-infested river. He only just managed to find a foothold and pull himself up the bank as Tschiffely clung on for dear life.

Two and a half years after setting out from Buenos Aires, Tschiffely reached Washington, D.C. He had achieved his lifelong ambition.

"I could never have done it," he said, "without Mancha and Gato. My two pals have shown powers of resistance to every hardship."

Tschiffely was given a hero's welcome, even meeting President Coolidge in the White House. Admirers suggested that the horses should live in a city park. But Tschiffely took Mancha and Gato back to Argentina and set them free. ❖

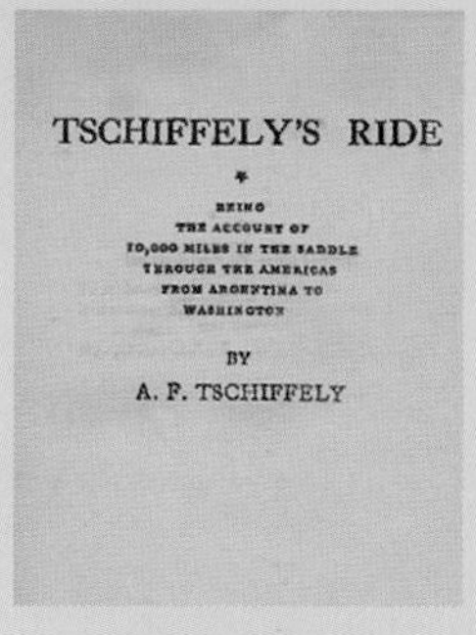
TSCHIFFELY'S RIDE

BEING
THE ACCOUNT OF
10,000 MILES IN THE SADDLE
THROUGH THE AMERICAS
FROM ARGENTINA TO
WASHINGTON

BY
A. F. TSCHIFFELY

**Tschiffely's Ride**
Now a famous man, Aimé Tschiffely wrote a book about his adventures.

**Born free**
Horses who grow up in the country can become sad and listless if confined in a city.

# Hollywood hero

In 1932 a star was born. He was a beautiful golden color with a white, flowing mane and tail. Son of a palomino mare and a racehorse, Golden Cloud was to become the most famous horse of his day.

**Movie town**
The 1930s was the golden age of filmmaking in Hollywood, California.

Golden Cloud made his big screen debut in 1938. His owners, Hudkin Stables, lent him out to play a part in the Hollywood film *The Adventures of Robin Hood*.

Later that year, Republic Studios decided to make a series of Westerns featuring the singing cowboy actor, Roy Rogers. They brought several horses round for Roy to audition. He fell for Golden Cloud the moment he climbed on to the horse's back.

**First part**
In the film, *The Adventures of Robin Hood*, Golden Cloud played Maid Marion's trusty steed, complete with medieval costume.

**Perfect partners**
Roy Rogers was called the King of the Cowboys, and Trigger soon became known as the Smartest Horse in the Movies.

**Famous pose**
Trigger's most spectacular feat was rearing up on his back legs with Roy Rogers on his back.

While they were making their first film, *Under Western Stars*, Golden Cloud was renamed "Trigger" because he was so quick.

Roy loved Trigger so much that after their third film, he bought Trigger for $2,500. From then on, they became full-time partners.

**Expensive**
Trigger was a true Hollywood horse. His silver saddle cost $50,000 and was set with 1,000 rubies.

**Starring role**
One of Trigger's best-loved movies was *Under California Stars* made in 1948. In this film, Trigger is stolen by thugs.

Trigger loved the camera. He often stole the show from Roy Rogers with a well-timed yawn or a graceful dance step.

He knew over 60 tricks. He could walk 150 steps on his hind legs, stamp his hoof to count, and draw a gun from a holster.

Trigger became one of the most popular characters in show business. He starred in 87 films and 101 TV shows, and once even had a party in the Grand Ballroom of the Astor Hotel in New York City.

*Trigger presents his passport on arrival in England in 1954.*

Like a true star, Trigger made special personal appearances. He always traveled in style, carried his own horse-sized passport, and signed his name with an X in hotel registers.

Trigger finally retired in 1957, and died in 1965, aged 33. Roy Rogers was heartbroken. He said he had lost "the greatest horse who ever came along." ❖

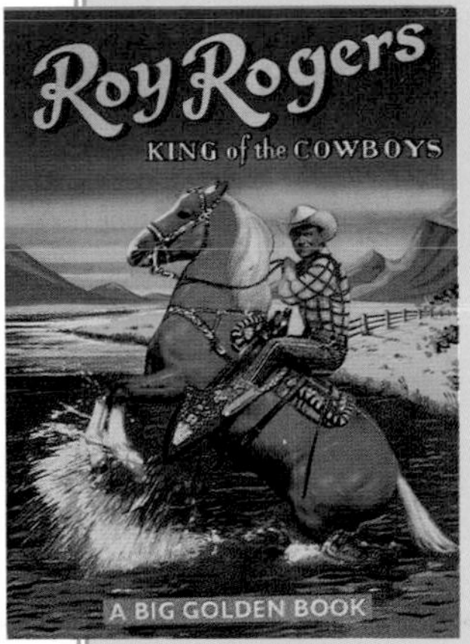


**Fan club**
Trigger's fan club produced hundreds of books and toys for its members.

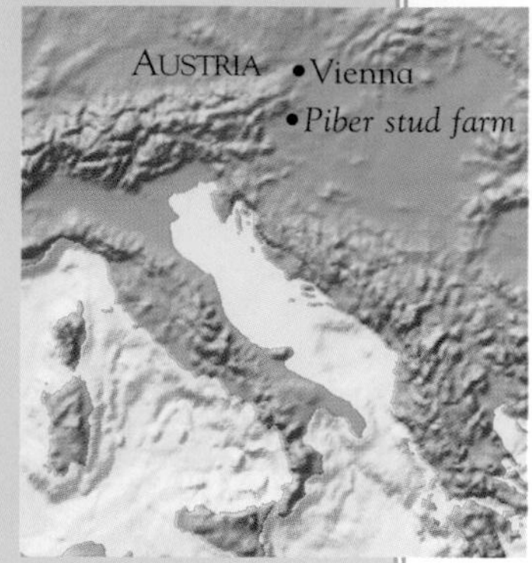


# Ballet on horseback

"He's a lively one," said the stable lad, pointing toward the dark colt leading the race across the field.

The colt's name was Favory. He was one of the Lipizzaner foals born in the early 1980s at the Piber stud farm, where horses are bred for the Spanish Riding School.

**Vienna**
The Spanish Riding School of Vienna, Austria, was founded in 1572. It is called "Spanish" because the original horses in the school were from Spain.

*Lipizzaner foals, or young horses, run free on the Piber stud farm.*

"Look how much energy he's got," said the stable lad.

"Maybe too much," said one of the grooms. Favory was popular with the workers at the stud farm, but could he make it at the school? The groom knew that if Favory was going to perform at the school's regular displays, he had to have personality, discipline, and strength.

**Lipizzaner**
The school's horses are Lipizzaners. They are descended from six stallions, one of which was called Favory. His descendants are always given his name.

*Lipizzaners are born dark but usually turn dazzling white when they are two years old.*

**Arena**
The grand Winter Riding Hall was built in 1735 by Emperor Charles VI of Austria. His portrait hangs at the far end of the arena.

When Favory was three and a half years old his training began.

He traveled with the other new students to Vienna. Here in the school's Winter Riding Hall, horses train and perform dressage, a set of complicated steps that have been the same for centuries. The school is famous worldwide for how skillfully its horses can do dressage.

Hardest of all the steps are the "Airs above the ground," a series of amazing jumps that only the strongest horses can perform.

All the riders at the school were eager to see if any of the new students were strong and steady enough to make the grade.

Unfortunately, Favory didn't give a good first impression. He broke away from his groom and galloped around the hall, showing off.

"We've got our work cut out with that one," said one of the riders.

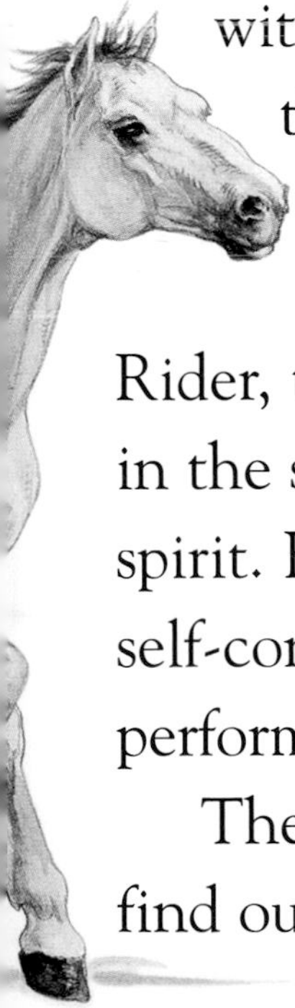

Watching Favory closely was the First Chief Rider, the most experienced rider in the school. He liked horses with spirit. But did Favory have the self-control that he would need to perform the Airs?

There was only one way to find out.

**Riders**
Riders join the school as teenagers and spend six years training.
A Chief Rider must have taught at least one horse the Airs.

**Costume**
In performance, riders wear cocked hats, tailcoats, and high black boots.

**In-hand**
A lunge rope is used to teach a horse to move in a controlled way and to obey the voice of his master.

The First Chief Rider decided to train Favory himself. He wanted to get the best out of Favory without changing his unique character.

For the first two weeks, the First Chief Rider led Favory gently by hand. Then he put a saddle on Favory and trained him on a rope called a lunge.

Favory hated the saddle, so the First Chief Rider only put it on for a few minutes at a time. Soon Favory let the First Chief Rider get on the saddle and ride him.

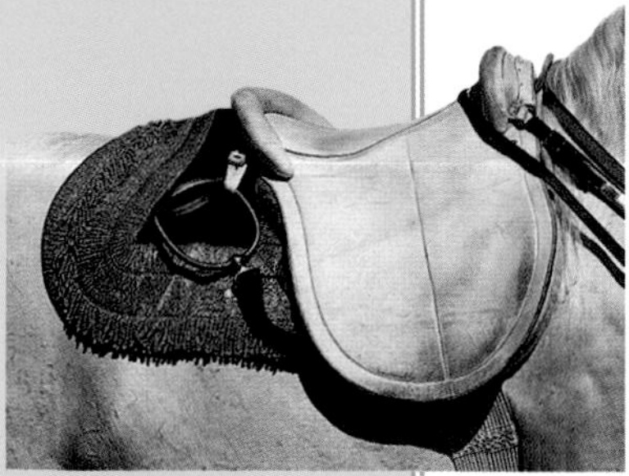

**Equipment**
The school has its own saddler to maintain the tack (saddles and bridles), some of which is hundreds of years old. Saddles are traditionally made out of white deerskin.

Then the First Chief Rider taught Favory how to focus his energy into performing dressage steps.

In just a few years, Favory was good enough to perform in the dressage section of the school's shows.

The school's sell-out shows are famous all over the world. The horses and riders perform dressage, the Airs, and a ballet to music.

The First Chief Rider was pleased with Favory's progress in the shows. Now it was time for the hardest task of all—to teach Favory the Airs.

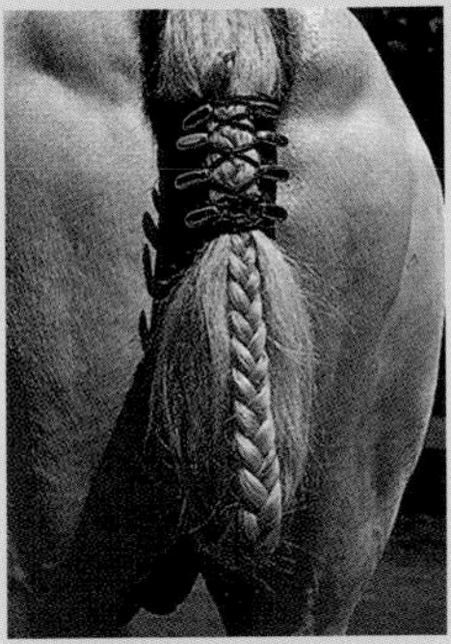

**Back view**
Lipizzaners' tails may be braided for performances.

**Levade**
(Lev-ard)
The horse raises his front legs up to 6 feet (2 meters) off the ground.

**Courbette**
(Caw-bet)
This involves jumping forward in the *Levade* position.

The first Air that Favory learned was the *Levade*. He had to rear up and balance on his hind legs.

Strongly built horses go on to learn the *Courbette*. But Favory's lively personality made him ideally suited to the *Capriole*.

To perform this spectacular Air, Favory had to leap up with all four feet off the ground. Then, at the highest point of the jump he had to kick his back legs out behind him.

Favory practiced the Airs until he could do them perfectly every time. It was not long before the First Chief Rider gave him a wonderful reward.

As the show draws to a close, the First Chief Rider presents a fully trained stallion to demonstrate the *Capriole*. It must be a stallion with great talent and a calm mind.

"Let's go," said the First Chief Rider one evening to the stallion that he had chosen.

The audience gasped as a magnificent white horse trotted gracefully to the center of the arena.

It was Favory. At last he had the chance to show off his skills. He performed the Airs to perfection and the audience loved him. Favory was a star. ❖

**Capriole**
(Cap-ree-ol)
This movement was developed for army horses to scare their enemies on the battlefield. It is often done in performance on a lunge rope.

**British Isles**
Paddy came from Ireland, a country that is famous for horse breeding.

**Skewbald**
Paddy was a drafthorse—a heavy working horse. His coat was brown and white, which is called skewbald.

# Royal drum horse

"We'll call him Paddy," said the farmer's wife. "After all, he was born on St. Patrick's Day, wasn't he?"

Her five children leaned over the fence to get a better look at the newborn foal in their field in Ireland. He had a beautiful brown and white coat and looked up at them with big dark eyes.

It was the early 1960s. In a couple of years, Paddy grew up into a fine, strong horse who enjoyed joining in the children's games—even the noisy ones. Their favorite game was to march with Paddy in procession, banging toy drums.

When Paddy was old enough to start work, he traveled to Edinburgh in Scotland. He began a new life pulling a milk cart for milkman Willie Wilson.

**Holyroodhouse**
The queen stays here rather than Edinburgh Castle, because the castle is drafty and uncomfortable.

One of the many busy streets they delivered milk to included Holyroodhouse. This is where the queen of England stays on royal visits to Edinburgh.

**Scots Guards**
The parade soldiers were Scots Guards, who perform ceremonial duties for the queen. Their band plays the bagpipes.

One morning, Willie found their milk route blocked by the color and noise of a royal parade.

He grabbed hold of Paddy's reins in case the parade frightened him, but Paddy didn't move a single muscle—not even when the big drums passed just in front of his nose. Boom! Boom!

**The queen**
Queen Elizabeth and her husband Philip, Duke of Edinburgh, make visits all over Great Britain.

"Look, there's the queen," whispered Willie, seeing who was in the big car following the parade.

A short time later, an amazing message arrived from the queen's Household Cavalry.

It said that they were looking for horses who could deal calmly with noisy situations.

A colonel of the Household Cavalry had spotted Paddy standing absolutely still, and thought he might make a good parade horse.

Paddy was soon on his way to the Royal Mews at Buckingham Palace in London. Here he met his new trainer, Corporal of the Horse Barry McKie, at the Life Guards.

**Life Guard**
The Life Guards are part of the Household Cavalry, the queen's bodyguard. They wear white horsehair plumes in their helmets.

**New home**
Household Cavalry horses live in stables in central London. They go to the Royal Mews for special occasions.

The Life Guards gave Paddy a new name, Cicero. He began the months of careful training that would turn him into a royal Drum Horse.

It would be his job to walk at the head of the parade carrying the Drum Master and two big drums.

No wonder the Life Guards needed a horse who wasn't bothered by noise!

**Drum beats**
When the army fought on horseback, drums were used to send messages and raise spirits. Now Drum Horses only take part in royal parades.

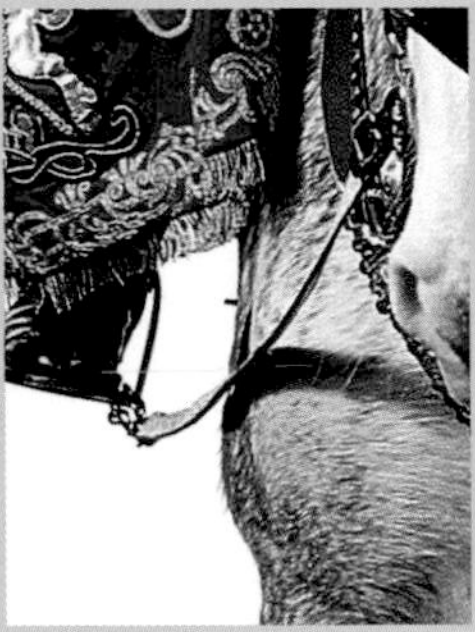

**Foot reins**
A Drum Horse is steered by reins attached to his rider's feet. During parades the rider uses his hands to play.

Cicero's first public appearance was on the queen's birthday in 1969. Thousands of people crowded the streets around Buckingham Palace. Cicero proudly led the marching band up the famous avenue called Horse Guard's Parade.

Cicero became one of the longest-serving royal Drum Horses ever, retiring after ten years in 1979. ❖

**Priceless**
The Guards' silver drums date from 1830. They weigh 118.5 pounds (53 kilograms).

**Celebration**
The queen's birthday parade is called the Trooping of the Color. The queen takes a salute from her troops, then leads them to Buckingham Palace up Horse Guard's Parade.

# Against all odds

"Come on, boy!" shouted Tim Molony over the clamor of horses' hooves.

Molony was watching Red Rum, the young horse he had recently bought, running in his first race in Liverpool in 1966.

Red Rum had started slowly, but was now gaining on the leaders. Could he catch them?

Molony had bought the Irish-born bay colt at auction for well under the asking price. He knew he'd gotten a good deal, but the question was how good?

As the race entered its final stretch, Red Rum speeded up toward the leading horse. His powerful legs pushed him faster and faster. With his last stride, he crossed the finishing line in a "dead heat," tying for first place with another horse.

**Great Britain**
Red Rum was born in Ireland but was moved all around Britain during his career.

**Horse auction**
At an auction, buyers bid against each other for the horse they want. An auctioneer controls the bidding until a price is reached.

In the next few years Red Rum won many more races and his career took off.

He was sold to a new owner. In Ripon, Yorkshire, Red Rum was looked after by a kind stable girl. She gave him his favorite treats—peppermints and carrots—whenever he ran well.

But the stable girl soon noticed that "Rummy" had a problem. He had a bone disease in his hooves that could mean the end of his career.

**Mom and Dad**
Red Rum was a Thoroughbred, a breed famous for speed. His dam (mother) was called *Mared* and his sire (father) was called *Quorum*, hence Red Rum.

*Red Rum (left) dead heats with Curlicue in his first race, the 1966 Thurby Selling Plate.*

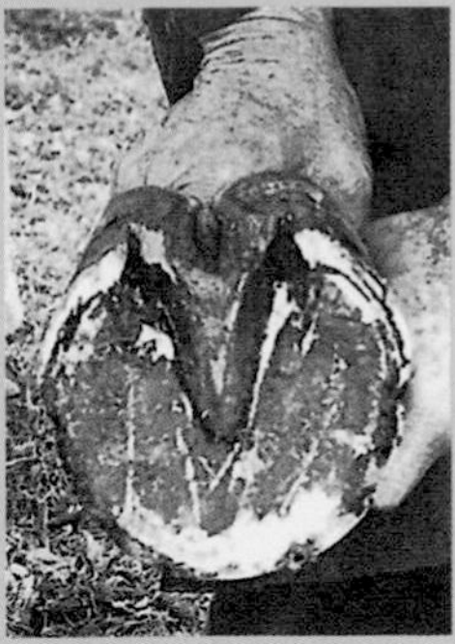

**Diseased**
The underside of Red Rum's hoof was riddled with bone disease. The poor horse was "unsound," meaning lame.

In 1972 Red Rum was sold to trainer Ginger McCain, who had stables at Southport, on the coast of northwest England.

Red Rum had seemed fit when Ginger bought him. But on his first day out on the beach with the other horses, Ginger realized that something was wrong.

"I've bought a lame horse!" he shouted. "Get him into the sea. We'll try saltwater on his legs."

What happened next saved Red Rum's career.

As Red Rum came out of the sea he seemed to be moving more easily.

"Look, he's trotting sound," said Ginger with a wide grin.

Running on the sand and cooling off in the sea was the perfect treatment for Red Rum's problem.

By the next spring, the once-lame horse was fit for the most challenging horse race of all, the Grand National.

**Sand and sea**
The salty sea water cleaned and cooled Red Rum's injured feet. He loved to run on sand because it was level and unchanging.

*Red Rum (in front) goes for a run on Southport Sands.*

**Race course**
The National is run at Aintree, near Liverpool, in April of every year. The race is 4.5 miles (7.2 kilometers) long.

Thirty-eight runners lined up to start the Grand National that April day in 1973. The ground was firm, just as Red Rum liked it.

In homes all over Britain, millions of television viewers settled down to enjoy the annual race.

Suddenly the horses were away!

**Becher's Brook**
There are 30 big fences to jump in the National. Becher's Brook is 6 feet (2 meters) high.

Thirty-eight powerful animals galloped at top speed toward the winning post.

Crisp took an early lead, with Red Rum back in twelfth place.

Red Rum gradually crept up the field, until, soaring over a fence, he found himself in second place.

Crisp and Red Rum were now a long way ahead of the chasing pack.

"And it's Crisp, Crisp in the lead from Red Rum, but Red Rum is making ground on him!" said the announcer.

Many horses would have settled for second place, but not Red Rum. Crisp was beginning to tire, and with each enormous stride, Red Rum was gaining on him.

"Red Rum! It's Red Rum! Red Rum has snatched it from Crisp!" shouted the announcer excitedly, as Red Rum crossed the finish line in first place.

**Photo finish**
The National is one of the most demanding races in the world. It tests a horse's speed and jumping ability, and also his stamina. After 30 jumps, there is a long gallop to the finish line.

**First prize**
The prize for winning the Grand National was a gold cup and more than $42,500.

**Statue**
A statue of Red Rum was built for Aintree, to celebrate its greatest victor. It was unveiled in 1988.

Not only had Red Rum won the Grand National, but he had set a new record time of nine minutes, 1.9 seconds. He had run at a speed of nearly 29 miles (46 kms) per hour.

Red Rum was a national hero.

The next year Red Rum entered the race again and amazingly won it for the second time. He was runner-up in 1975 and 1976, before winning it for a staggering third time in 1977, when he was 12 years old.

No other horse has won the race three times. It is a record unlikely ever to be beaten.

*Red Rum attends the unveiling of his statue.*

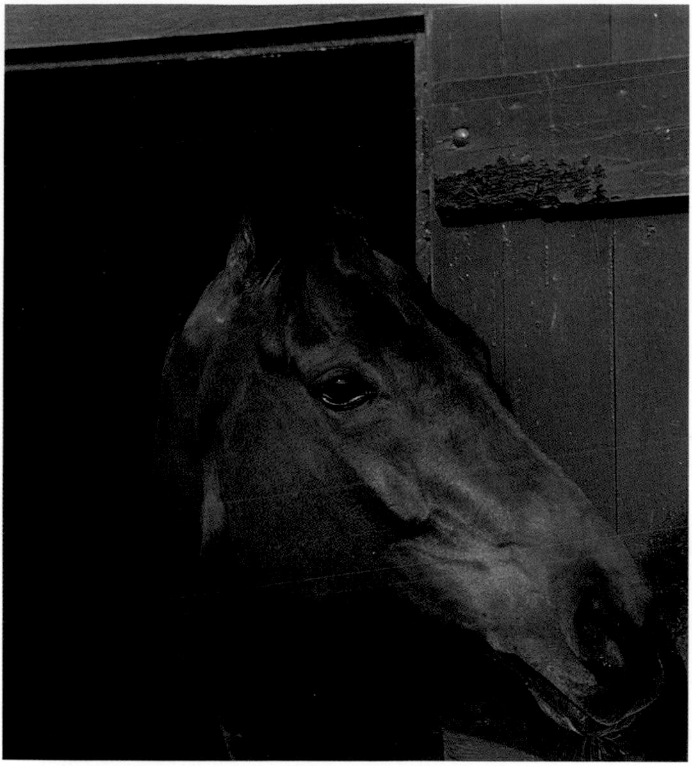

A few years later, Red Rum retired from racing and began a new life as a celebrity. He attended the opening of supermarkets, and many other events, as a star guest.

Red Rum died in 1995 at the age of 30. He is buried in a grave next to the finish line at Aintree, where he had his greatest triumphs. Fans visit to pay tribute to an amazing horse who overcame such great odds to become a racing hero. ❖

**Easy to spot**
In his work as a celebrity, Red Rum always wore his famous sheepskin noseband.

**Sunny shadow**
On sunny days, the shadow of the winning post at Aintree falls on Red Rum's grave.

# The horse family

Horses and ponies belong to the same family as donkeys, wild asses, and zebras. This is called the Equid (ECK-wid) family.

In the wild, horses live in herds on open grasslands. They use speed to escape from their enemies, and newborn foals can get up and run within an hour of being born.

Horses form strong bonds with other members of their herd. This loyalty is easily transferred to a human owner.

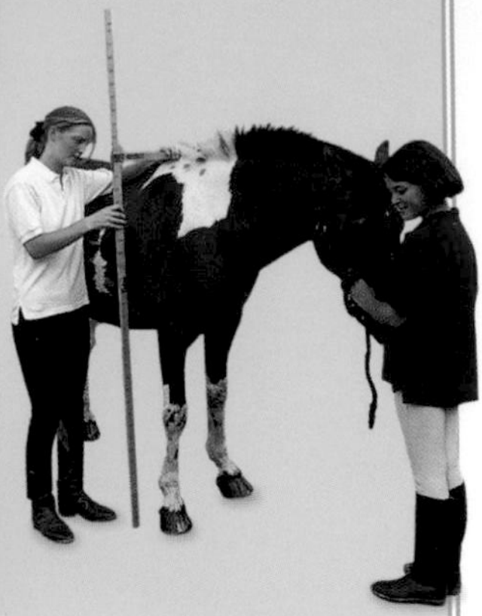

**Hands high**
The height of a horse is measured in "hands." One hand is the width of an adult's hand—about 4 inches (10 cm).

Domestic horses come in many different shapes and sizes, but there are three main types—heavy horses, light horses, and ponies. Heavy horses are the largest and can measure over 67 inches (168 cm) high. Ponies are the smallest and always measure under 58 inches (147 cm).

The oldest breed of horse is the Przewalski (perz-uh-VOL-skee) horse, which comes from Mongolia in Asia. It is the only living link with the wild ancestors of today's horses and ponies. ❖

*Przewalski horse*

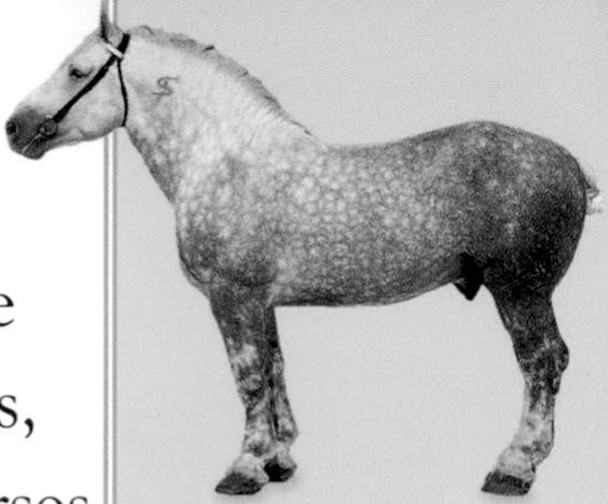

**Heavy horse**
Heavy horses are tall and have broad, strong shoulders.

**Light horse**
Light horses have narrow bodies, long legs, and sloped shoulders.

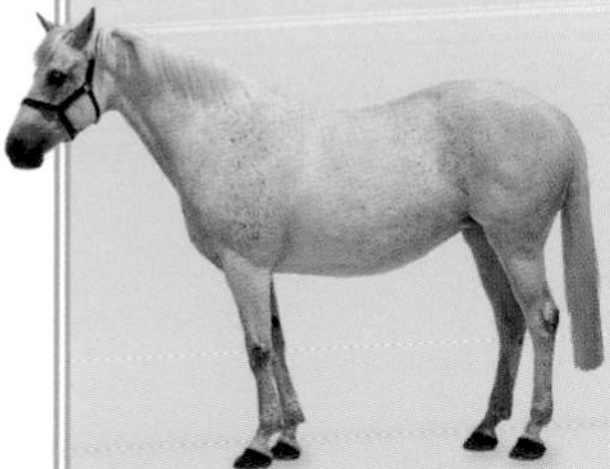

**Pony**
Ponies have shorter legs in relation to their bodies than light and heavy horses.

# Glossary

**Ambition**
Something that is strongly desired.

**Ambush**
A surprise attack made from a hiding place.

**Arena**
An enclosed space for large shows and sporting events.

**Bay**
A horse with a reddish coat and black mane, tail, legs, ears, and nose.

**Ceremonial occasion**
A special occasion on which a series of acts is carried out to celebrate the occasion.

**Chasing pack**
The group of horses behind the leaders in a horse race.

**Colt**
A young male horse.

**Continent**
One of the earth's large land masses, i.e., Africa, Antarctica, Asia, Australia, Europe, North America, and South America.

**Detour**
A route taken when another route is blocked.

**Gorge**
A deep valley, often with a river running through it.

**Groom**
A person who looks after horses.

**Lame**
Having an injured leg or foot that causes a limp. Limping is walking unevenly.

**Mosquito**
A small winged insect that bites.

**Palomino**
A horse with a gold-colored coat and a white mane and tail.

**Parade**
A procession of people, and often a band, to celebrate a special occasion.

**Passport**
An official paper given to a person by the government so that the person can be identified in a foreign country.

**Quicksand**
A deep, wet bed of sand that sucks down anything on its surface.

**Relay**
A system where fresh runners or horses are posted at intervals along a route. Each member of a relay team runs only one part of the route.

**Runner-up**
The person or horse that finishes second in a race or competition.

**Salute**
Raising the right hand to the forehead to show respect.

**Stagecoach**
A horse-drawn passenger coach that travels a regular route.

**Stallion**
A fully grown male horse that can be used for breeding.

**Stamina**
The strength to keep on going.

**Telegraph**
A system for sending messages over long distances. It uses electronic signals sent through a wire.

**Trotting sound**
To run slowly and smoothly without limping.

**Vampire bat**
A bat from Central or South America that lives on the blood of other animals.

**Western**
A film about cowboys in the western United States, especially during the time of exploration.

**White House**
The large white building which is home to the president of the United States in Washington, D.C.